50 Cozy Casserole Recipes for Summer

By: Kelly Johnson

Table of Contents

- Classic Chicken and Rice Casserole
- Cheesy Broccoli and Rice Casserole
- Beef and Bean Enchilada Casserole
- Vegetable Lasagna Casserole
- Tuna Noodle Casserole
- Baked Ziti with Mozzarella and Basil
- Creamy Mushroom and Spinach Casserole
- Sausage and Pepper Casserole
- Sweet Potato and Black Bean Casserole
- Chicken Pot Pie Casserole
- Stuffed Bell Pepper Casserole
- Shepherd's Pie with Mashed Potatoes
- Buffalo Chicken Casserole
- Ham and Cheese Breakfast Casserole
- Cabbage Roll Casserole
- Eggplant Parmesan Casserole
- BBQ Chicken and Corn Casserole
- Chili Mac and Cheese Casserole
- Spinach and Ricotta Casserole
- Italian Sausage and Zucchini Casserole
- Coconut Curry Cauliflower Casserole
- Pasta Primavera Casserole
- Crack Chicken Casserole
- Beef Stroganoff Casserole
- Baked Potato Casserole with Cheese
- Mushroom and Barley Casserole
- Pulled Pork Casserole with Coleslaw
- Cheesy Chicken and Broccoli Casserole
- Vegetable Quinoa Casserole
- Classic Macaroni and Cheese Casserole

- Teriyaki Chicken Casserole
- Spinach Artichoke Casserole
- Creamy Tomato and Basil Casserole
- Baked Ratatouille Casserole
- Sausage and Kale Casserole
- Caribbean Jerk Chicken Casserole
- Lentil and Vegetable Casserole
- Stuffed Shells Casserole
- Corn and Zucchini Casserole
- Cheesy Taco Casserole
- Green Bean Casserole with Crispy Onions
- Chicken and Biscuit Casserole
- Creamy Chicken Alfredo Casserole
- Teriyaki Beef and Rice Casserole
- Bacon and Spinach Egg Casserole
- Classic Shepherd's Pie with Ground Lamb
- Seafood Pasta Bake
- Zucchini and Tomato Gratin Casserole
- Pea and Ham Casserole
- Baked Chicken Fajita Casserole

Classic Chicken and Rice Casserole

Ingredients

- 2 cups cooked chicken, shredded
- 1 cup rice
- 2 cups chicken broth
- 1 can cream of mushroom soup
- 1 cup frozen peas and carrots
- Salt and pepper to taste

Instructions

1. Preheat the oven to 350°F (175°C).
2. In a large bowl, mix together the chicken, rice, chicken broth, soup, peas, carrots, salt, and pepper.
3. Pour the mixture into a greased baking dish and cover with foil. Bake for 30-40 minutes or until heated through.

Cheesy Broccoli and Rice Casserole

Ingredients

- 2 cups cooked rice
- 2 cups broccoli florets
- 1 cup cheddar cheese, shredded
- 1 can cream of chicken soup
- 1/2 cup milk

Instructions

1. Preheat the oven to 350°F (175°C).
2. In a bowl, combine rice, broccoli, cheese, soup, and milk. Mix well.
3. Transfer to a greased baking dish and bake for 25-30 minutes until bubbly.

Beef and Bean Enchilada Casserole

Ingredients

- 1 pound ground beef
- 1 can black beans, drained
- 1 can enchilada sauce
- 8 corn tortillas, cut in half
- 2 cups shredded cheese

Instructions

1. Preheat the oven to 375°F (190°C).
2. In a skillet, cook the ground beef until browned. Drain excess fat.
3. In a baking dish, layer tortillas, beef, beans, enchilada sauce, and cheese. Repeat layers, ending with cheese.
4. Bake for 25-30 minutes until heated through and cheese is melted.

Vegetable Lasagna Casserole

Ingredients

- 9 lasagna noodles, cooked
- 2 cups ricotta cheese
- 2 cups marinara sauce
- 2 cups mixed vegetables (zucchini, spinach, mushrooms)
- 2 cups mozzarella cheese, shredded

Instructions

1. Preheat the oven to 375°F (190°C).
2. In a baking dish, layer noodles, ricotta, vegetables, marinara sauce, and mozzarella. Repeat layers, finishing with mozzarella.
3. Bake for 30-35 minutes until bubbly and golden.

Tuna Noodle Casserole

Ingredients

- 2 cups cooked egg noodles
- 1 can tuna, drained
- 1 can cream of mushroom soup
- 1 cup frozen peas
- 1 cup shredded cheese

Instructions

1. Preheat the oven to 350°F (175°C).
2. In a large bowl, mix together noodles, tuna, soup, peas, and half of the cheese.
3. Pour into a greased baking dish, top with remaining cheese, and bake for 25-30 minutes.

Baked Ziti with Mozzarella and Basil

Ingredients

- 1 pound ziti pasta, cooked
- 2 cups marinara sauce
- 2 cups mozzarella cheese, shredded
- 1/2 cup grated Parmesan cheese
- Fresh basil leaves, for garnish

Instructions

1. Preheat the oven to 375°F (190°C).
2. In a baking dish, combine cooked ziti and marinara sauce. Top with mozzarella and Parmesan cheese.
3. Bake for 25-30 minutes until cheese is melted and bubbly. Garnish with fresh basil before serving.

Creamy Mushroom and Spinach Casserole

Ingredients

- 2 cups cooked rice
- 2 cups fresh spinach
- 1 cup mushrooms, sliced
- 1 can cream of chicken soup
- 1/2 cup sour cream
- 1 cup shredded cheese

Instructions

1. Preheat the oven to 350°F (175°C).
2. In a bowl, mix rice, spinach, mushrooms, soup, sour cream, and cheese.
3. Pour into a greased baking dish and bake for 25-30 minutes until heated through.

Let me know if you need more recipes or any adjustments!

Sausage and Pepper Casserole

Ingredients

- 1 pound Italian sausage, sliced
- 2 bell peppers, sliced (any color)
- 1 onion, sliced
- 1 can diced tomatoes (14.5 oz)
- 1 teaspoon Italian seasoning
- Salt and pepper to taste

Instructions

1. Preheat the oven to 375°F (190°C).
2. In a skillet, brown the sausage over medium heat. Add bell peppers and onion; cook until tender.
3. Stir in diced tomatoes, Italian seasoning, salt, and pepper. Transfer to a greased baking dish and bake for 25-30 minutes.

Sweet Potato and Black Bean Casserole

Ingredients

- 2 large sweet potatoes, peeled and diced
- 1 can black beans, drained and rinsed
- 1 cup corn (frozen or canned)
- 1 teaspoon cumin
- 1 teaspoon chili powder
- 1 cup shredded cheese (cheddar or Monterey Jack)

Instructions

1. Preheat the oven to 400°F (200°C).
2. In a bowl, combine sweet potatoes, black beans, corn, cumin, and chili powder.
3. Transfer to a greased baking dish, top with cheese, and bake for 30-35 minutes until sweet potatoes are tender.

Chicken Pot Pie Casserole

Ingredients

- 2 cups cooked chicken, shredded
- 1 cup frozen mixed vegetables
- 1 can cream of chicken soup
- 1 cup milk
- 1 package refrigerated pie crusts

Instructions

1. Preheat the oven to 375°F (190°C).
2. In a bowl, mix chicken, vegetables, soup, and milk.
3. Pour mixture into a greased baking dish, top with pie crust, and bake for 30-35 minutes until crust is golden.

Stuffed Bell Pepper Casserole

Ingredients

- 4 bell peppers, chopped
- 1 pound ground beef or turkey
- 1 cup cooked rice
- 1 can diced tomatoes (14.5 oz)
- 1 teaspoon Italian seasoning
- 1 cup shredded cheese

Instructions

1. Preheat the oven to 375°F (190°C).
2. In a skillet, brown the meat; drain excess fat. Stir in rice, tomatoes, and seasoning.
3. Mix in chopped peppers, transfer to a greased baking dish, top with cheese, and bake for 25-30 minutes.

Shepherd's Pie with Mashed Potatoes

Ingredients

- 1 pound ground beef or lamb
- 1 cup frozen peas and carrots
- 1 onion, chopped
- 2 cups mashed potatoes (prepared)
- 1 tablespoon Worcestershire sauce
- Salt and pepper to taste

Instructions

1. Preheat the oven to 400°F (200°C).
2. In a skillet, brown the meat with onion; drain fat. Stir in vegetables, Worcestershire sauce, salt, and pepper.
3. Transfer meat mixture to a baking dish, top with mashed potatoes, and bake for 20-25 minutes until heated through.

Buffalo Chicken Casserole

Ingredients

- 2 cups cooked chicken, shredded
- 1 cup buffalo sauce
- 1 cup ranch dressing
- 2 cups cooked pasta
- 1 cup shredded cheese

Instructions

1. Preheat the oven to 350°F (175°C).
2. In a bowl, combine chicken, buffalo sauce, ranch dressing, and pasta.
3. Transfer to a greased baking dish, top with cheese, and bake for 25-30 minutes until cheese is bubbly.

Ham and Cheese Breakfast Casserole

Ingredients

- 6 eggs
- 1 cup milk
- 2 cups diced ham
- 1 cup shredded cheese (cheddar or Swiss)
- 1 cup diced bread
- Salt and pepper to taste

Instructions

1. Preheat the oven to 350°F (175°C).
2. In a bowl, whisk together eggs and milk. Stir in ham, cheese, bread, salt, and pepper.
3. Pour into a greased baking dish and bake for 30-35 minutes until set.

Let me know if you need more recipes or any adjustments!

Cabbage Roll Casserole

Ingredients

- 1 pound ground beef or turkey
- 1 onion, chopped
- 1 head of cabbage, chopped
- 1 can diced tomatoes (14.5 oz)
- 2 cups cooked rice
- 1 teaspoon Italian seasoning
- Salt and pepper to taste

Instructions

1. Preheat the oven to 375°F (190°C).
2. In a skillet, brown the meat with onion; drain excess fat.
3. Stir in chopped cabbage, tomatoes, rice, seasoning, salt, and pepper.
4. Transfer to a greased baking dish and bake for 30-35 minutes until the cabbage is tender.

Eggplant Parmesan Casserole

Ingredients

- 2 large eggplants, sliced
- 3 cups marinara sauce
- 2 cups shredded mozzarella cheese
- 1 cup grated Parmesan cheese
- 1 teaspoon Italian seasoning

Instructions

1. Preheat the oven to 375°F (190°C).
2. Layer half of the eggplant in a greased baking dish; top with marinara, mozzarella, and Parmesan.
3. Repeat layers and sprinkle with Italian seasoning.
4. Bake for 30-40 minutes until bubbly and golden.

BBQ Chicken and Corn Casserole

Ingredients

- 2 cups cooked chicken, shredded
- 1 cup BBQ sauce
- 1 can corn, drained
- 1 cup shredded cheese
- 1 cup crushed tortilla chips

Instructions

1. Preheat the oven to 350°F (175°C).
2. In a bowl, mix chicken, BBQ sauce, corn, and half of the cheese.
3. Transfer to a greased baking dish, top with tortilla chips and remaining cheese, and bake for 20-25 minutes until heated through.

Chili Mac and Cheese Casserole

Ingredients

- 1 pound ground beef
- 1 can chili (15 oz)
- 2 cups cooked macaroni
- 2 cups shredded cheese
- 1 teaspoon chili powder

Instructions

1. Preheat the oven to 350°F (175°C).
2. In a skillet, brown the beef; drain excess fat.
3. Stir in chili, cooked macaroni, and chili powder.
4. Transfer to a greased baking dish, top with cheese, and bake for 20-25 minutes until cheese is melted.

Spinach and Ricotta Casserole

Ingredients

- 2 cups fresh spinach, chopped
- 1 cup ricotta cheese
- 1 cup marinara sauce
- 2 cups cooked pasta
- 1 cup shredded mozzarella cheese

Instructions

1. Preheat the oven to 375°F (190°C).
2. In a bowl, mix spinach, ricotta, marinara, and cooked pasta.
3. Transfer to a greased baking dish, top with mozzarella, and bake for 25-30 minutes until bubbly.

Italian Sausage and Zucchini Casserole

Ingredients

- 1 pound Italian sausage, sliced
- 2 zucchinis, sliced
- 1 onion, chopped
- 1 can diced tomatoes (14.5 oz)
- 1 cup shredded mozzarella cheese

Instructions

1. Preheat the oven to 375°F (190°C).
2. In a skillet, brown the sausage with onion; drain excess fat.
3. Stir in zucchini and tomatoes; transfer to a greased baking dish.
4. Top with mozzarella and bake for 25-30 minutes until cheese is melted.

Coconut Curry Cauliflower Casserole

Ingredients

- 1 head of cauliflower, cut into florets
- 1 can coconut milk (14 oz)
- 2 tablespoons curry powder
- 1 cup shredded cheese (optional)

Instructions

1. Preheat the oven to 375°F (190°C).
2. In a bowl, mix cauliflower, coconut milk, and curry powder.
3. Transfer to a greased baking dish and top with cheese if using.
4. Bake for 30-35 minutes until cauliflower is tender.

Let me know if you need any further adjustments or additional recipes!

Pasta Primavera Casserole

Ingredients

- 12 oz pasta (penne or rotini)
- 2 cups mixed vegetables (bell peppers, zucchini, carrots)
- 1 cup marinara sauce
- 1 cup shredded mozzarella cheese
- 1 teaspoon Italian seasoning

Instructions

1. Preheat the oven to 350°F (175°C).
2. Cook pasta according to package instructions; drain.
3. In a large bowl, mix cooked pasta, vegetables, marinara, and Italian seasoning.
4. Transfer to a greased baking dish, top with mozzarella, and bake for 25-30 minutes until cheese is bubbly.

Crack Chicken Casserole

Ingredients

- 2 cups shredded cooked chicken
- 1 packet ranch dressing mix
- 8 oz cream cheese, softened
- 1 cup shredded cheddar cheese
- 1 cup cooked bacon, crumbled

Instructions

1. Preheat the oven to 350°F (175°C).
2. In a bowl, combine chicken, ranch mix, cream cheese, half of the cheddar, and bacon.
3. Transfer to a greased baking dish, top with remaining cheddar, and bake for 20-25 minutes until heated through.

Beef Stroganoff Casserole

Ingredients

- 1 pound ground beef
- 1 onion, chopped
- 2 cups mushrooms, sliced
- 1 can cream of mushroom soup (10.5 oz)
- 2 cups egg noodles, cooked
- 1 cup sour cream

Instructions

1. Preheat the oven to 350°F (175°C).
2. In a skillet, brown the beef with onion and mushrooms; drain excess fat.
3. Stir in soup, cooked noodles, and sour cream; transfer to a greased baking dish.
4. Bake for 20-25 minutes until heated through.

Baked Potato Casserole with Cheese

Ingredients

- 4 large potatoes, peeled and diced
- 1 cup sour cream
- 1 cup shredded cheddar cheese
- 1/2 cup cooked bacon, crumbled
- 1/2 cup green onions, chopped

Instructions

1. Preheat the oven to 375°F (190°C).
2. Boil potatoes until tender; drain and mash slightly.
3. In a bowl, mix potatoes, sour cream, half of the cheese, bacon, and green onions.
4. Transfer to a greased baking dish, top with remaining cheese, and bake for 25-30 minutes until cheese is melted.

Mushroom and Barley Casserole

Ingredients

- 1 cup pearl barley
- 2 cups vegetable broth
- 2 cups mushrooms, sliced
- 1 onion, chopped
- 2 cups spinach
- 1 teaspoon thyme

Instructions

1. Preheat the oven to 350°F (175°C).
2. In a skillet, sauté mushrooms and onion until soft.
3. In a baking dish, combine barley, broth, sautéed vegetables, spinach, and thyme.
4. Cover and bake for 50-60 minutes until barley is tender.

Pulled Pork Casserole with Coleslaw

Ingredients

- 2 cups pulled pork
- 1 cup BBQ sauce
- 2 cups coleslaw mix
- 1 cup shredded cheddar cheese
- 1 cup cornbread mix

Instructions

1. Preheat the oven to 350°F (175°C).
2. In a bowl, mix pulled pork with BBQ sauce.
3. In a greased baking dish, layer pulled pork, coleslaw, and half of the cheese.
4. Top with cornbread mix and remaining cheese, then bake for 30-35 minutes until heated through.

Cheesy Chicken and Broccoli Casserole

Ingredients

- 2 cups cooked chicken, shredded
- 2 cups broccoli florets, steamed
- 1 can cream of chicken soup (10.5 oz)
- 1 cup shredded cheddar cheese
- 1 cup cooked rice

Instructions

1. Preheat the oven to 350°F (175°C).
2. In a bowl, combine chicken, broccoli, soup, half of the cheese, and rice.
3. Transfer to a greased baking dish, top with remaining cheese, and bake for 25-30 minutes until bubbly.

Let me know if you need any more recipes or adjustments!

Vegetable Quinoa Casserole

Ingredients

- 1 cup quinoa, rinsed
- 2 cups vegetable broth
- 2 cups mixed vegetables (zucchini, bell peppers, carrots)
- 1 can diced tomatoes (14.5 oz)
- 1 teaspoon Italian seasoning

Instructions

1. Preheat the oven to 350°F (175°C).
2. In a pot, combine quinoa and broth; bring to a boil, then reduce heat and simmer for 15 minutes.
3. In a bowl, mix cooked quinoa, vegetables, tomatoes, and seasoning.
4. Transfer to a greased baking dish and bake for 25-30 minutes until heated through.

Classic Macaroni and Cheese Casserole

Ingredients

- 2 cups elbow macaroni
- 2 cups shredded cheddar cheese
- 1 cup milk
- 1/4 cup butter, melted
- 1/4 cup breadcrumbs

Instructions

1. Preheat the oven to 350°F (175°C).
2. Cook macaroni according to package instructions; drain.
3. In a bowl, mix cooked macaroni, cheese, milk, and melted butter.
4. Transfer to a greased baking dish, top with breadcrumbs, and bake for 20-25 minutes until bubbly.

Teriyaki Chicken Casserole

Ingredients

- 2 cups cooked chicken, shredded
- 1 cup teriyaki sauce
- 2 cups cooked rice
- 1 cup mixed vegetables (peas, carrots)
- 1 cup shredded mozzarella cheese

Instructions

1. Preheat the oven to 350°F (175°C).
2. In a bowl, combine chicken, teriyaki sauce, rice, and vegetables.
3. Transfer to a greased baking dish, top with mozzarella, and bake for 20-25 minutes until cheese is melted.

Spinach Artichoke Casserole

Ingredients

- 2 cups fresh spinach, chopped
- 1 can artichoke hearts, drained and chopped
- 1 cup cream cheese, softened
- 1/2 cup sour cream
- 1 cup shredded mozzarella cheese

Instructions

1. Preheat the oven to 350°F (175°C).
2. In a bowl, mix spinach, artichokes, cream cheese, sour cream, and half of the mozzarella.
3. Transfer to a greased baking dish, top with remaining mozzarella, and bake for 20-25 minutes until bubbly.

Creamy Tomato and Basil Casserole

Ingredients

- 2 cups cooked pasta (penne or rotini)
- 1 can crushed tomatoes (28 oz)
- 1 cup heavy cream
- 1/2 cup fresh basil, chopped
- 1 cup shredded parmesan cheese

Instructions

1. Preheat the oven to 350°F (175°C).
2. In a bowl, combine cooked pasta, crushed tomatoes, cream, and basil.
3. Transfer to a greased baking dish, top with parmesan, and bake for 25-30 minutes until heated through.

Baked Ratatouille Casserole

Ingredients

- 1 zucchini, sliced
- 1 eggplant, diced
- 1 bell pepper, diced
- 1 can diced tomatoes (14.5 oz)
- 1 teaspoon thyme

Instructions

1. Preheat the oven to 375°F (190°C).
2. In a baking dish, layer zucchini, eggplant, bell pepper, and tomatoes.
3. Sprinkle with thyme, cover with foil, and bake for 30-35 minutes until vegetables are tender.

Sausage and Kale Casserole

Ingredients

- 1 pound Italian sausage, cooked and crumbled
- 4 cups kale, chopped
- 1 cup ricotta cheese
- 1 cup marinara sauce
- 1/2 cup shredded mozzarella cheese

Instructions

1. Preheat the oven to 350°F (175°C).
2. In a bowl, mix sausage, kale, ricotta, and marinara.
3. Transfer to a greased baking dish, top with mozzarella, and bake for 25-30 minutes until heated through.

Let me know if you need more recipes or any adjustments!

Caribbean Jerk Chicken Casserole

Ingredients

- 2 cups cooked chicken, shredded
- 1/2 cup jerk seasoning
- 2 cups cooked rice
- 1 can black beans (15 oz), drained and rinsed
- 1 cup corn (fresh or frozen)
- 1 cup shredded cheddar cheese

Instructions

1. Preheat the oven to 350°F (175°C).
2. In a bowl, mix chicken, jerk seasoning, rice, black beans, and corn.
3. Transfer to a greased baking dish, top with cheddar cheese, and bake for 25-30 minutes until heated through.

Lentil and Vegetable Casserole

Ingredients

- 1 cup lentils, rinsed
- 2 cups vegetable broth
- 1 onion, diced
- 2 carrots, diced
- 2 cups mixed vegetables (zucchini, bell peppers)
- 1 teaspoon thyme

Instructions

1. Preheat the oven to 350°F (175°C).
2. In a pot, combine lentils and vegetable broth; bring to a boil, then simmer for 30 minutes until tender.
3. In a bowl, mix cooked lentils, onion, carrots, vegetables, and thyme.
4. Transfer to a greased baking dish and bake for 20-25 minutes until heated through.

Stuffed Shells Casserole

Ingredients

- 20 jumbo pasta shells, cooked and drained
- 2 cups ricotta cheese
- 1 cup shredded mozzarella cheese
- 2 cups marinara sauce
- 1/4 cup grated Parmesan cheese

Instructions

1. Preheat the oven to 350°F (175°C).
2. In a bowl, mix ricotta and half of the mozzarella.
3. Stuff each shell with the ricotta mixture and place in a greased baking dish.
4. Pour marinara sauce over the shells and top with remaining mozzarella and Parmesan.
5. Bake for 25-30 minutes until bubbly.

Corn and Zucchini Casserole

Ingredients

- 2 cups corn (fresh or frozen)
- 2 zucchinis, shredded
- 1 cup cornmeal
- 1 cup milk
- 2 eggs, beaten
- 1 teaspoon baking powder

Instructions

1. Preheat the oven to 350°F (175°C).
2. In a bowl, mix corn, zucchini, cornmeal, milk, eggs, and baking powder.
3. Transfer to a greased baking dish and bake for 30-35 minutes until set and golden.

Cheesy Taco Casserole

Ingredients

- 1 pound ground beef or turkey
- 1 packet taco seasoning
- 2 cups tortilla chips
- 1 can diced tomatoes with green chilies (14.5 oz)
- 2 cups shredded cheese (cheddar or Mexican blend)

Instructions

1. Preheat the oven to 350°F (175°C).
2. In a skillet, cook the ground meat until browned; drain excess fat.
3. Stir in taco seasoning and tomatoes.
4. In a greased baking dish, layer tortilla chips, meat mixture, and cheese.
5. Bake for 20-25 minutes until cheese is melted.

Green Bean Casserole with Crispy Onions

Ingredients

- 4 cups fresh green beans, trimmed
- 1 can cream of mushroom soup (10.5 oz)
- 1 cup milk
- 1 teaspoon soy sauce
- 1 cup crispy fried onions

Instructions

1. Preheat the oven to 350°F (175°C).
2. In a pot, boil green beans until tender; drain.
3. In a bowl, mix soup, milk, soy sauce, and half of the crispy onions.
4. Stir in green beans and transfer to a greased baking dish.
5. Top with remaining onions and bake for 25-30 minutes until bubbly.

Chicken and Biscuit Casserole

Ingredients

- 2 cups cooked chicken, shredded
- 1 can cream of chicken soup (10.5 oz)
- 1 cup milk
- 1 cup frozen mixed vegetables
- 1 can refrigerated biscuit dough

Instructions

1. Preheat the oven to 375°F (190°C).
2. In a bowl, mix chicken, soup, milk, and vegetables.
3. Pour mixture into a greased baking dish.
4. Cut biscuit dough into quarters and place on top of the mixture.
5. Bake for 25-30 minutes until biscuits are golden and cooked through.

Let me know if you need more recipes or any adjustments!

Creamy Chicken Alfredo Casserole

Ingredients

- 3 cups cooked pasta (penne or rotini)
- 2 cups cooked chicken, shredded
- 2 cups Alfredo sauce
- 1 cup broccoli florets
- 1 cup shredded mozzarella cheese

Instructions

1. Preheat the oven to 350°F (175°C).
2. In a bowl, mix cooked pasta, chicken, Alfredo sauce, and broccoli.
3. Transfer to a greased baking dish and top with mozzarella cheese.
4. Bake for 25-30 minutes until heated through and cheese is bubbly.

Teriyaki Beef and Rice Casserole

Ingredients

- 1 pound ground beef
- 2 cups cooked rice
- 1 cup teriyaki sauce
- 1 cup mixed vegetables (carrots, peas, bell peppers)
- 1/2 cup green onions, chopped

Instructions

1. Preheat the oven to 350°F (175°C).
2. In a skillet, cook ground beef until browned; drain excess fat.
3. Stir in teriyaki sauce and mixed vegetables; cook for 5 minutes.
4. In a greased baking dish, combine beef mixture and cooked rice.
5. Bake for 20-25 minutes, garnished with green onions before serving.

Bacon and Spinach Egg Casserole

Ingredients

- 6 eggs
- 1 cup milk
- 1 cup cooked bacon, crumbled
- 2 cups fresh spinach
- 1 cup shredded cheddar cheese

Instructions

1. Preheat the oven to 350°F (175°C).
2. In a bowl, whisk together eggs and milk.
3. Stir in bacon, spinach, and cheddar cheese.
4. Pour mixture into a greased baking dish and bake for 30-35 minutes until set.

Classic Shepherd's Pie with Ground Lamb

Ingredients

- 1 pound ground lamb
- 1 onion, diced
- 2 carrots, diced
- 2 cups mashed potatoes
- 1 cup beef broth
- 1 teaspoon thyme

Instructions

1. Preheat the oven to 400°F (200°C).
2. In a skillet, cook ground lamb, onion, and carrots until lamb is browned.
3. Stir in beef broth and thyme; simmer for 10 minutes.
4. Transfer meat mixture to a baking dish and top with mashed potatoes.
5. Bake for 25-30 minutes until golden on top.

Seafood Pasta Bake

Ingredients

- 2 cups cooked pasta (fusilli or shells)
- 1 cup shrimp, peeled and deveined
- 1 cup crab meat
- 2 cups Alfredo sauce
- 1/2 cup grated Parmesan cheese

Instructions

1. Preheat the oven to 350°F (175°C).
2. In a bowl, combine cooked pasta, shrimp, crab meat, and Alfredo sauce.
3. Transfer to a greased baking dish and sprinkle with Parmesan cheese.
4. Bake for 25-30 minutes until heated through.

Zucchini and Tomato Gratin Casserole

Ingredients

- 3 zucchinis, sliced
- 2 cups cherry tomatoes, halved
- 1 cup breadcrumbs
- 1 cup shredded mozzarella cheese
- 1 teaspoon Italian seasoning

Instructions

1. Preheat the oven to 375°F (190°C).
2. In a bowl, combine zucchini, tomatoes, breadcrumbs, and Italian seasoning.
3. Transfer to a greased baking dish and top with mozzarella cheese.
4. Bake for 30-35 minutes until bubbly and golden.

Pea and Ham Casserole

Ingredients

- 2 cups frozen peas
- 1 cup diced ham
- 1 can cream of mushroom soup (10.5 oz)
- 1 cup milk
- 1 cup shredded cheese (cheddar or Swiss)

Instructions

1. Preheat the oven to 350°F (175°C).
2. In a bowl, mix peas, ham, soup, and milk.
3. Pour into a greased baking dish and top with cheese.
4. Bake for 25-30 minutes until bubbly.

Baked Chicken Fajita Casserole

Ingredients

- 2 cups cooked chicken, shredded
- 1 bell pepper, sliced
- 1 onion, sliced
- 1 packet fajita seasoning
- 1 cup shredded cheese
- 4 tortillas, cut into strips

Instructions

1. Preheat the oven to 350°F (175°C).
2. In a skillet, sauté bell pepper and onion until tender.
3. In a bowl, combine chicken, vegetables, fajita seasoning, and tortilla strips.
4. Transfer to a greased baking dish and top with cheese.
5. Bake for 25-30 minutes until heated through.

Let me know if you need more recipes or modifications!

www.ingramcontent.com/pod-product-compliance
Lightning Source LLC
LaVergne TN
LVHW081334060526
838201LV00055B/2640